KANDINSKY

KANDINSKY

TEXT BY

MARCEL BRION

HARRY N. ABRAMS, INC. · PUBLISHERS
NEW YORK

LIBRARY OF CONGRESS CATALOG CARD NUMBER : 61–11 937
PUBLISHED IN THE UNITED STATES OF AMERICA, 1961. ALL RIGHTS
RESERVED. NO PART OF THE CONTENTS OF THIS BOOK MAY BE
REPRODUCED WITHOUT THE WRITTEN PERMISSION OF THE PUBLISHERS,
HARRY N. ABRAMS, INC., NEW YORK
PRINTED IN GERMANY

INTRODUCTION

When he wrote that form "is subjective content in an objective envelope," Kandinsky himself indicated the approach we should adopt when we look at his painting and attempt to evaluate and understand it. The unity of the two components of a work of art – the painting itself and the emotion that gave birth to it – is stated here. The inward meaning gives life and body to the created object; the spectator who ignores or misinterprets this meaning perceives nothing but the interplay of masses and colors. The full message of Kandinsky's painting is revealed only to one who recognizes the spiritual identity of the form and the initial emotion that inspired it. To convey his intended meaning, each emotion demands its appropriate and exclusive language. Thus Kandinsky's technique is itself in perpetual motion, constantly changing so that it can more precisely follow and represent the movement of his thought and feeling.

The close relationship of this technique with the development of Kandinsky's aesthetic and philosophic position is clear to those who realize that his paintings must be looked at not merely as plastic phenomena, but rather as "occurrences" in which soul, sensibility, restlessness, and fantasy cooperate to the same end. The unity of his work throughout all its chronological development, from the first Moscow pictures to the final "great synthesis" of the years 1934–1944, is not destroyed by the customary division into periods, which is justified by the need to characterize by their distinctive features the marked variations within each stage of his development. This division does not produce an impression of discontinuity, because the links between the periods clearly show the almost biological determinism that governs his work as a whole, as surely as phase follows phase in the life of an organism.

When in 1911 Franz Marc wrote to August Macke, "The closer I get to Kandinsky, the more I learn to appreciate him," he expressed clearly the attitude of anyone who continually strives to reach the heart of Kandinsky's creation. Each picture is not only an adventure of the feelings and the spirit, but also a technical and aesthetic adventure. Although so many important branches of contemporary painting are derived from Wassily Kandinsky's work or have been inspired by it, his achievement is particularly significant in relation to the whole of abstract art. The part that he played in the birth of abstraction and in its development is established historically by the dates of his first abstract works, while an understanding of its various currents can be gained by studying the internal and external modifications of non-representational form in his own paintings.

Always free from the burden of naturalism, Kandinsky's style began as "poetic pictorialism"; through his experiments, which were of great importance for him and for all modern art, he ended by creating an entirely autonomous, complete universe, possessing its own natural laws, its own atmosphere

6

and even its own physiological properties. ["For me every dot, every line, whether still or in motion, becomes alive and offers me its soul,"] wrote Kandinsky in his autobiographical work, *Rückblicke (Backward Glances)*, his confession as man and as artist. Kandinsky's paintings offer their souls to us; it is for us to seek out their soul, in form, beyond form, but always by means of form.

EXPLORATION OF THE WORLD
OF MYSTERY AND LIGHT

From his youth, according to Kandinsky himself, the maxim that dominated and directed his work was "to express mystery in terms of mystery." This concept never ceased to inspire the evolution of his art. Though there are broad and sweeping changes in his treatment of form and space and in his technical methods—from the poetic realism of 1900 to the autonomous universes in motion of his "Parisian period" compositions—there remains a stylistic unity that is connected with this controlling theme. It corresponds to everything that was most noble, sincere, and original in his artistic personality. His was a world of mysteries woven of enigmas, disguised behind the problematical life of forms. From his childhood, which was probably more packed with incident than most ordinary childhoods, this mysterious world had been part of Kandinsky's philosophy and aesthetic and had influenced his attitude towards beings and objects. If a person's youth can be measured by his capacity for wonderment, Kandinsky remained forever young. The last pictures painted in his Parisian period, when he was almost eighty, display his eternally youthful taste for the joyful astonishment afforded him by those dazzling constellations of moving, thrilling, nervous forms that peopled the canvases of the "great synthesis" from 1934 to 1944.

His childhood impressions of the wonderful fairyland of Moscow, with its multi-colored striped church domes and bustling, teeming, happy markets, its colorful extravaganza of crowds of good-humored people described by Stravinsky in *Petrouchka*—the gossiping peasant women, the coachmen, the peasants with their stiff blouses and baggy trousers—remained part of Kandinsky's character. These recollections merged with something more intimate and less obvious: the indefinable emotions that stirred in his unconscious as the legacy of distant atavisms. In Russia the East is never far away; in Kandinsky's ancestry, Mongolia was still recent, with its memories of nomad princes living in brilliant, many-colored tents, surrounded by strange, precious, shining objects. The painter has set down a miscellany of conscious memories in *Backward Glances,* published in 1913. To these must be added the riches, dimly surmised rather than clearly perceived, of his ancestral background, which always seemed to Kandinsky very close. He would never have felt the need for a universal communion that bordered on theosophy and anthroposophy, which he expressed in *On the Spiritual in Art,* had he not recognized his kinship with the ancient lineage of the Khans.

From his early youth the painter was in love with "Mother Moscow," that magical town so full of contrasts. The splendid and unique aspects of that city were so deeply impressed on his sensibility that his enchantment re-appears in "period" after "period," under guises that for all their differences are always related by the firm, interior unity that controls them. This spell, which surrounds him like an aura, makes its influence felt in three equally important fields: in his passion for color, in the magic of fables, and in the importance of objects charged

PROMENADE. 1901
COLLECTION DR. Z. GOLDBERG, ZURICH

with supernatural vitality that lend themselves to transformation into symbols. He also had a rather undefined sense of Slavonic messianism as preached by Soloviev, who foresaw Moscow as "the Third Rome"; and he was convinced that art was the only effective means of establishing harmonious relations between man and things.

"In the beginning was color." These are the opening words of Kandinsky's memoirs; and he continues by describing the primary palette of his childish emotions. "The first colors to make a great impression on me were light bright green, white, carmine, black, and yellow ochre. My memories of these go back to the age of three. The colors belong to various different objects, which I cannot remember as clearly as the colors themselves." He bought his first box of paints when he was only thirteen, but his understanding of the world was based upon its color characteristics long before his vocation as an artist became apparent. Red was the exuberant spirit of joyful vitality, of melodious well-being; in Russian, the same word serves for both "red" and "beautiful." In contrast, black aroused a fear close to repugnance and horror. As a child, he wished for a happy world peopled with gaily striped objects whose colors would never change; the reality of an object was inherent in its color rather than in its form. Visual sensations dominated all others; he even conceived music in terms of color, while tactile sensations played little part in his exploration of the world around him.

His predilection for color naturally inclined the young Kandinsky's imagination towards the enchanted kingdom of fairy tales. His spirit was exceptionally receptive to the strange and the supernatural, and he was readily captivated by the poetic fantasy and glistening variety of color in these stories. Old Russia was well stocked with fables, legends, splendid epics, and wonder-working heroes. In the eyes of a child and of the Russian people, the exploits of a historical personage, Ilya Mourometz for example, and those of a legendary paladin, are equally real. It was natural and spontaneous for Kandinsky's first paintings to take their themes and, even more, their atmosphere, from this truly Russian fantasy, which was so captivating and tyrannical that years later, in Munich, Kandinsky was still painting his Russian soul and the Moscow air. His memories of legendary Russia are represented in his

BRIDGE AT KOCHEL. 1902
STEDELIJK MUSEUM, AMSTERDAM

woodcuts and in paintings like *Sunday* (1904), *Arrival of the Merchants* (1905), *Troïka* (1906), and *Panic, Storm Bell* and *Motley Life* (all of 1907). They are rendered in a naive and rustic style that shows the influences of the vigorous carving and violent colors of popular wood engravings mingled with the lyrical refinements of the Jugendstil. The realism of this first period is in fact unreal: it is a musical unreality, where emotions stir in the twilight of legend, an unreality which, while the images and themes of Russia recede, pervades wooded groves where unexpressed passions lie. Here, investigating the

11

mystery does not result in elucidating but rather in deepening it. *Promenade* (1901), *Bright Air* (1902) and *Trysting Place, No. 2* (1903) preserve a kind of enigmatic grace that demands the resonance of color to be *listened to* like an intimate symphony, or as if it were chamber music, collected and gathered within itself, enclosed in its own mystery.

This mystery, the product of the artist's imagination and of those marvelous fables whose beauty and strangeness are equally unfathomable, attaches itself to objects. It is important for us to understand the passion that Kandinsky as a very small child had for a dun-colored toy horse, with which he liked to play. It would be tempting to connect this sort of child's game with the horse theme in the vast composite myth of Nordic religions, in which the horse, endowed with supernatural faculties, appears as a sacred creature, sometimes ritually sacrificed, and whose function is often to accompany the dead on their voyage to the other world. This fantastic aspect of the horse appears repeatedly in the engravings of Baldung Grien and Dürer, the drawings of Goya, and the paintings of Fuseli, Stubbs, Delacroix, and Géricault. The theme appears in Kandinsky's work after the *Rider* (1903), an extraordinary romantic canvas in which a dream horse gallops through the outskirts of a forest across an unreal landscape. *Crusader* (1903), *Riding Couple* (1903), *Lancer in Landscape* (1906), *Troïka* (1906), *Rider* (1909), *Painting with Archer* (1909), the *Diabolical Horsemen* (1911) and the numerous variations on the motif of St. George all show that before 1910, during his representational period, the painter was attracted to the horse. At about the same time Franz Marc, also captivated by the animal world and the supernatural power that animated it, was painting his blue horses. In 1911 the two painters were instrumental in founding a publication—an almanac—*Der Blaue Reiter* (Blue Rider),

12

for which artists, poets, and musicians collaborated; the group also organized exhibitions that became landmarks in the history of modern art.

The Blue Rider movement was one of the boldest and most fruitful attempts to free European painting from naturalism and the academic. Contemporaneous with tendencies that advocated painting having purely plastic values, it offered an intensely beautiful poetic content. When the various sketches Kandinsky made for the Almanac are examined, one can clearly perceive the assertion and accentuation of his tendency towards abstraction. It was already evident in the famous "historical" watercolor of 1910, sometimes called abstract, sometimes concrete – both adjectives being used in the same sense. The rider, who up to then had belonged to a "story," from this moment is freed from it completely; the horse theme, which was frequently associated with the mountain theme, as in *Blue Mountain* (1909), *Rider on a Mountain Top, Improvisation 9* (1910), favored the transition from a representational to an almost abstract form, which now became pure energy.

The mad ride of the horsemen behind the mountainous peaks of *With the Sun* (1910) is already symptomatic of the disintegration of form as such that reaches its culmination in the "dramatic" period of 1910–1919, when the process of abstraction becomes more and more absolute, ending in the total elimination of all possible reference to objects in nature. Even when remaining to a certain extent involved in a story, the rider, especially in the 1903 painting, is part of the landscape: he carries the landscape with him in his gallop. Kandinsky had a passion for movement. His pictures are always in movement, eternally self-creating, disturbed by the mobility of deep undersea currents that endow the forms with an extraordinary

SUNDAY. 1904
BOYMANS-VAN BEUNINGEN MUSEUM, ROTTERDAM

capacity for constant change. In less than ten years, this passion for motion led Kandinsky to abolish the too limited, too explicit story-telling actuality of the horseman, who had haunted and obsessed him from his youth, and who represented, far more than a childhood memory, a strange personal attribute of the painter; he now became the inspiration of a rhythmic arabesque, a seismograph of passion, the gesture of an impassioned spirit.

The forms of the horse and the rider, the mountain and the surrounding countryside, blend into one another. In the speed and synthesis of *Lyrical* (1911) or the rich symphony of *Improvisation 21 (with Yellow Horse)* 1911, forms and colors are composed around the arc across the picture's surface traversed by the leaping horse, the symbol of speed and energy.

14

PARK OF ST. CLOUD (WITH RIDER). 1906
COLLECTION NINA KANDINSKY, PARIS ▷

Kandinsky here realizes the ambition of his contemporaries, the Italian Futurists, which was to incorporate movement into the picture and make of it "something in motion." He did this without recourse to the divisionist technique of Balla, Boccioni, or Severini, simply by eliminating from the painting everything but movement. His predilection for the horse helped him in this process of stripping away all that was not in itself movement; the change from representational to abstract form was largely made thanks to the horse, which already incorporated in its gallop the whole dynamic structure of the picture.

The background of Russian ballads, German legends, and popular fables gives a strange appearance to those paintings that date before 1907. But this atmosphere with its quaint, graceful crinolines allows us to perceive the basis of this type of descriptive art: it is actually a device for clothing with objective forms structures built on the action and interaction of rhythms. Kandinsky soon realized that neither object nor subject matter was necessary any longer; how the process of their removal was achieved will be seen later. For the present, it is sufficient to compare two paintings typifying opposing tendencies—the *Duel* of 1902 and the large abstract mural composition painted in 1922 for the jury-free exhibition in Berlin. The striking analogies between them make us realize that, in Kandinsky's mind, the terms of the aesthetic vocabulary, "abstract" or "concrete," "representational" or "non-representational," are no more than verbal exercises. The first of these two pictures, a color drawing on a black ground, unquestionably *represents* two horsemen charging at each other with lances; in the abstract composition of twenty years later, the descriptive qualities of the figures and their morphological characteristics have fallen away like an outer garment. In this Berlin composition, only a bare, dynamic understructure re-

16

mains, clothed in non-representational forms that are even more fantastic than the trappings of Tartar paladins worn by the heroes of the 1902 drawing.

It is almost impossible to imagine Kandinsky painting a still life; even the static elements in the landscapes and compositions of his representational period are constructions of movement rather than structures in movement; the interplay of twisting curves in the color drawing, *Skating* (1910), is already almost abstract. As his figures become increasingly the symbols of a vital spatial movement (*Composition II,* 1910; *Composition IV,* 1911; *Improvisation 12,* 1910; *Composition I,* 1910), the horse and horseman become even further dematerialized. If the subjects can sometimes still be recognized in the completely abstract compositions after 1911, they are only elements of a dynamic draftsmanship that does not "represent" anything other than its own rhythm. In the same way and for the same reason, in the "architectural" works of the Bauhaus period (1922–1933), the boat themes—hull, funnel, masts, and sails—are converted into geometrical forms, but these "abstractions" are still animated and inspired by the fresh sea breeze that Kandinsky loved so much.

The sparkling golden and colored cupolas of Mother Moscow, the joyful kaleidoscope of Odessa, to which Kandinsky's family moved a few years after his birth, account for his perpetual enchantment with everything that moved or glowed with color. The old Russia of Kandinsky's Russian paintings and Remizov's "round-eyed" wonderment is difficult to imagine today; it was still the "holy capital of the universe," home of a chosen people to whom Soloviev entrusted the glory and responsibility of establishing the millennium of the Third Rome.

Kandinsky's family expected him to enter the legal profession, for which he studied and prepared while he painted. It

17

RAINBOW AT MURNAU. 1909
STÄDTISCHE GALERIE, MUNICH

was in fact as a jurist that he was sent on a mission to the
province of Vologda in 1889 to study the peculiarities of
peasant law; he took advantage of this mission to delve into
the popular art of the region. In *Backward Glances* he has
recounted his remarkable journey through forests, across steppes
and great frozen rivers, and told his surprise at finding villages
"whose inhabitants were, without exception, either clothed in

gray, with faces and hair of a yellowish green, or in contrast arrayed in an extraordinary variety of many-colored striped costumes, looking like paintings come to life and walking on two legs." In the *isbahs,* all the furnishings were decorated in brilliant colors, and Kandinsky experienced the strange feeling of "finding myself surrounded on every side by Painting, as if I myself had become part of Painting."

The trip to Vologda decided his vocation, for although assiduous enough in his legal work, he realized his true calling, and instead of accepting the professorship of law at the University of Dorpat offered to him in 1896, he left for Munich, where he took courses in art with Azbé and Stuck and made the acquaintance of Jawlensky, Klee, and Marc. He has said that he derived his most profitable lessons from the palette itself rather than from his masters. "The palette, product of the components that make up a painting, is itself often more beautiful than any painting. It should be appreciated for the pleasure that it produces. It seems to me that the living soul of colors emits a musical sound when the inflexible will of the artist's brush snatches part of their life away. Sometimes I hear the colors whispering as they mix; it is like a mysterious experience surprisingly occurring during the magical experiments of an alchemist." There are words in the Russian language for expressing sensations of color that are lacking in any other language. The experience of color Kandinsky had already begun in Russia was broadened in Bavaria and continued to nourish the essential purpose of his art, which was to raise form to its maximum strength and lightness in brilliance and in vivacity of color.

At an exhibition of the French Impressionists, Kandinsky came face to face with Monet's *Haystacks.* He was disturbed, for the picture posed the problem of representation in painting.

19

Had the artist a right to treat the object in any way he pleased, with no consideration for verisimilitude? Kandinsky carried the experiment beyond the point reached by the Impressionists (further than which, in fact, they could not go) and eliminated the object altogether. He realized the ultimate result of carrying the Impressionist procedure to its logical conclusion, *non-objectivity*.

At this period, however, there was no question of abstract painting. Kandinsky could not work according to a formal program, as did the Cubists. If painting were ever to rid itself of representation, it would be by the operation of light and

IMPROVISATION 3. 1909
COLLECTION NINA KANDINSKY, PARIS

SKETCH FOR COMPOSITION II. 1909
SOLOMON R. GUGGENHEIM, NEW YORK

color, and not through research into geometrical form as carried out by Malevitch or the Dutch De Stijl group (both, at this period, still obstinately representational). The Impressionist exhibition, which had moved Kandinsky "in his inmost being," completely freed him from the Russian realism of Repine that he had formerly admired; acquaintance with the Rembrandts in the Hermitage taught him the importance of a "time continuum" in a painting. He very quickly comprehended the peculiar attitude toward time that characterized the Dutch

21

master and especially his work—his chiaroscuro, the orchestration of the different "musical parts," and their interplay.

The pre-eminence of sheer painting, burning with the spiritual feeling that inspired it but freed from all traces of story-telling, painting that in its means of expression comes close to music and led Kandinsky to suggest a parallel between Rembrandt and Wagner, could only be the result of a liberating operation that would follow the trail blazed by the Impressionists but impose a new ethic. The most important question raised by a study of Monet's *Haystacks* is the legitimacy of suppressing the represented object. The *raison d'être* of this painting is not the stack but rather the complex of colored forms inspired by the sight of the stacks, representing them, perhaps, but not reproducing them. Could one not just as well eliminate the stack as an object, retaining it as form?

In *Backward Glances* Kandinsky says that the fact that he did not distinguish the haystack "disturbed and irritated" him. He asked himself "if the painter had the right to paint in such an imprecise way," and he felt that "this work lacked a subject." At that period, he admits, he was aware only of naturalistic art; the idea that a picture has no need of a subject, that it is self-sufficient, that a painting is a thing-in-itself on which no narrative need be embroidered, was a complete reversal of the painter's aesthetic. Later, he came under the influence of the strong non-realist currents that were stirring in Russian and German painting around 1900. The style of the Ballets Russes and the Jugendstil interested him by their novelty, their boldness, and the way in which they played freely with forms and colors, refusing to be bound by the circumscribed tradition of representation that was faithful to objective reality.

The great break did not occur at this juncture, however, and for some time longer Kandinsky continued to like and depict the

RAILROAD NEAR MURNAU. 1909
STÄDTISCHE GALERIE, MUNICH

subject. But the first step towards absolute freedom had been taken, in so far as the subject became purely poetic, enchanted, and unreal; it was the artist who decided to what extent the painting should be endowed with "magical power." He was forty-four when, in 1910, he painted his first abstract water-color; there was no element of caprice in his choice of non-representational art, nor was it the result of a sudden burst of enthusiasm. The lesson derived in 1895 from the *Haystacks* had had time in which to bear fruit. His choice (which, it must be remembered, was also a spiritual turning point) was not prompted by mere willfulness. From what we know of his pictures of 1900, for example the portrait of Maria Krushchov reproduced in Grohmann's excellent monograph (p. 257), Kandinsky was established as a very good figure painter, already much preoccupied with harmonizing his subject, style, and medium, the relationship among which was the focus of his research. Henceforth every experiment in European painting finds its echo in Kandinsky's art. The radical transformation of form that was taking place simultaneously in France, Russia, and Germany was realized in his work also. This transformation, the attainment and conquest of contemporary art, is a denial of tradition, the invention of another concept of space and time – in fact, many highly diversified concepts – and of a new, young, rich, fresh sense of the painter's medium. Above all, it is a new code governing the relation between the artist and the object, the artist and his work. Even in Kandinsky's work during his pre-abstract period (ending approximately in 1910), a remarkable number of pictorial discoveries of great interest and rich potentialities are evident. In his quasi-mythical scenes of Old Russia, his use of broken strokes of color resulted in a quick, intense vibration that reinforced the fairy-tale character of a mediaeval world of dreams and legends and allowed a sort of romantic nostalgia to flow from the pictures. In Munich, where Kandinsky came to live in 1896, this nostalgia preserved his lost Russia, substituting for its actual landscapes his "Russia of the soul," which lived within him up to his last hours in Paris. This chromatic pointillism, found also in the temperas on black cardboard executed in Holland in 1904, was like a musical notation, no longer orchestrated in the manner of Wagner but with a tonal impressionism that was very Russian.

24

In Munich, where he worked with Azbé and Stuck, Kandinsky formed solid, fruitful friendships with Jawlensky, Klee, and Marc. Each in his own way envisaged that it might be possible somehow to eliminate the object; as Macke put it in 1907, "to combine colors on a panel without thinking of any real object," which was what Kandinsky had had at the back of his mind since 1895. Painting after nature disappointed him because increasingly the real object seemed to him to be a superfluous encumbrance; the contemplation of objective reality upset the arrangement of forms and colors generated and controlled by his inner self, independent of any observation of nature. This arrangement impressed him more and more emphatically as being the only justification for a painting. The memory of the "beautiful hour" just before dusk in Moscow, the splendid harmony of the reds, the surging symphony of the palette, soon reduced the objective landscape to a mere prop around which the composition could be organized. Invention prevailed over observation, and the same attempt to subordinate the object—even the painted object—to the painting itself can be seen developing in his Fauve landscapes done in 1909 at Murnau, which followed the unreal fairytale pointillism in the themes of Old Russia and Holland. Markedly different from the scientific Neo-Impressionist divisionism based on Chevreul's optical theories, Kandinsky's plastic divisionism is, like that of Klimt, purely emotional, of the feelings rather than of the senses, animated by the heart rather than by the eye. Both these approaches, which start from the same initial point but lead in opposite directions, are already abstract. The absence of titles from many of the canvases of the "dream landscapes" period, and their replacement by the characteristic words "improvisation" and "composition," stress their true, potential abstraction.

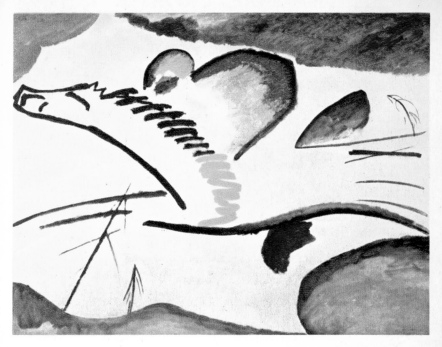

LYRICAL. 1911
BOYMANS-VAN BEUNINGEN MUSEUM, ROTTERDAM

The incident of the inverted picture, related by Kandinsky
in *Backward Glances,* finally confirmed his belief that he had
reached the goal "for which he had been unconsciously search-
ing, which was to break up the painted object and absorb it
into the painting." Henceforth he was unshakable in his conviction that "objects hinder my painting." The event took
place at Munich and was very important in the artist's life,
all the more so because he was mature and, in his mid-forties,
in the prime of life. "It was nearing dusk, and I had returned

home with my box of paints after doing a sketch, still engrossed in my dream and reflecting on the work I had accomplished, when I suddenly noticed on the wall a picture of extraordinary beauty, shining with an inner radiance. I stood dumbfounded, then I approached this pictorial enigma, in which I could see only forms and colors whose purport remained incomprehensible. It was one of my own pictures, which had been hung on the wall upside down!" Kandinsky's astonishment at seeing his picture as a new thing, the product of his instinct rather than of his will, corresponds with his habit of going outdoors to invent a picture rather than to study the landscape.

He might have been expected to dispense sooner with sketching from nature; that he did not do so was probably because he always loved nature passionately and appreciated it even more, he said, when he was not representing it. He was also attracted to nature because of the power that objective forms had to suggest and to instruct. Kandinsky always preferred the word "concrete" to the word "abstract" to designate a non-representational painting, emphasizing the non-intellectual (in the sense of non-cerebral) aspect of his art. He approached and left nature by the same path, that of sensation, for, as he said, "I could never employ forms proceeding from logical processes, but only those born within me by an inner necessity," i. e. imagined forms rather than factual data. His imagination played freely with sensations and the emotions that, even more than any actual shapes, were the result of his contact with nature. Kandinsky found permeating his researches and discoveries "an ordered system of spiritually active beings," through whose operation "dead matter becomes living spirit." Already his quest for the spiritual content of form was evident as the principal driving force behind an artistic creativity based on the invisible rather than the visible. It was another aspect of his aspiration towards the transcendental, which was to be increasingly asserted in succeeding years.

The Impressionist technique that set analytical brush strokes against unrealistic black backgrounds, the decidely unnaturalistic atmosphere of his legendary compositions, the Fauvist heightening of color enclosed in separate cells like the ancient Germanic enamels of the time of the barbarian invasions, the oriental love of color for its own sake, mark the stages of Kandinsky's detachment from the representation of nature. It was not detachment from nature itself, which for the artist was not the goal but only the means of reaching beyond nature.

Kandinsky set the final form of the problem of the object, which was simultaneously preoccupying the Cubists, Futurists, Fauves, and all who concluded that the ultimate potentialities of representation of nature for its own sake had been exhausted by Impressionism. The object, which – as he now realized – hindered his painting, must be transcended, after having been broken up. Non-objective art was liable to the danger of becoming merely ornamental and decorative. It was accordingly necessary to change the symbolism and give a new meaning to the word "object." The painter asked himself, "With what can the object be replaced?" The simultaneous attraction and shock implicit in these few words that were destined to revolutionize painting is evident from *Backward Glances*. Kandinsky no longer answered the questions of his day about the different new methods of treating the object by considering the object itself, but rather by considering what should replace it.

All the elements required as a basis for founding so-called abstract, or rather non-representational, painting are here. The way was open for the transition to the abstract. But Kandinsky was no cultist; he had been driven logically to his conclusion by his need to give the maximum inward life to his painting.

29

LANDSCAPE WITH TOWER. 1909
PRIVATE COLLECTION, PARIS

He understood the difficulties his solution would present to the artist and the public. Both would probably have equal trouble in assimilating this creative form; he knew the heavy demands that it imposed. Fifty years ago, he declared that representational and non-representational art could exist harmoniously side by side—since the two different modes of expression are both capable of satisfying the artist's deepest feelings, his spirituality even more than his aesthetic. "I do not feel that non-objective painting is a blow aimed at completely destroying the validity of all preceding art," he said. "I see it only as an inevitable, huge division of one of the limbs of the original old trunk, which has split into two chief branches, both contributing to the formation of 'the Living Tree' ... As far as I am concerned, I love every form of art that arises from spiritual necessity and is created by the spirit, just as I detest those that are not." Kandinsky here set forth clearly and authoritatively the principles of his artistic ethic and emphasized the theme he was to develop later in *Über das Geistige in der Kunst (On the Spiritual in Art)*.

In 1910, the painter reached what he called his "spiritual turning point" and completed his transition from the representational to the abstract – not suddenly, but rather as the result of a series of advances, during which the natural form of the object came to be ever more completely concealed within its spiritual form.

A SPIRITUAL TURNING POINT

The dramatic period, the years from 1910–1920, opened with the publication of a book that made as deep an impression as did Worringer's *Abstraktion und Einfühlung (Abstraction and Empathy)* which appeared almost at the same time. The publication of *On the Spiritual in Art* at the same period as the dramatic paintings was as striking as the later emergence of the "architectural" and "circle" paintings (during the period when Kandinsky was teaching at the Bauhaus) and the simultaneous appearance of his treatise *Punkt und Linie zu Fläche (Point and Line to Plane)*. Although the latter was in a sense a didactic work, it was also highly revealing of the evolution of

31

FIRST ABSTRACT WATERCOLOR. 1910
COLLECTION NINA KANDINSKY, PARIS

the artist's aesthetic and technique. The decade that opened
with the historic advent of the Blue Rider also saw him arrive
at a spiritual turning point – the expression is Kandinsky's own
– of exceptional importance. About 1910, as he was getting
close to this spiritual turning point, which he had already been
approaching in his mind and work for some years, his painting
was enriched by an independence of form and color essential
for this intimate fulfilment. The turning point corresponded to

the artist's need to turn inwards and pursue more deeply the demands of his intelligence and sensibility. In reality there was no sudden change; the various stages of the simultaneous evolution of spiritual content and plastic form resemble a gradual biological development, determined by inevitable organic unity, plastic creativity and the guiding idea that controls such aesthetic transformations.

It was about 1910, too, that a certain symbolism of forms appeared which, while becoming more and more flexible, less and less obvious, was to remain one of the constant factors in the Blue Rider period. The theme of the blue horseman and the mountain, frequently repeated in former years in a representational manner, progressively shed all anecdotal connotation, all deliberate and narrowly historical representation, to become a symbol free from fortuitous incidents and literary allusions. The rider became the group emblem of the almanac, *Der Blaue Reiter*, which appeared in 1911. Kandinsky discovered that, after having been liberated from literal symbolism to become a form that alluded to the subject rather than describing it, the symbol had still further to go: it was to become a form whose forcefulness depended principally on its denial of all direct plastic relationship with the image that had inspired it.

In the first variations on the horseman theme, the change from figure to symbol was nothing other than the plastic organization of emotion to attain its most moving expressive power. The new form no longer refers to anything but itself, to a concept without any reference to objects pre-existing in nature. It is a thing-in-itself, yet nevertheless repeats and confirms, increasingly clearly and vigorously, the "principle of inner necessity," keystone of all Kandinsky's work. "It is evident that color harmony depends upon effective communication," one reads in *On the Spiritual in Art*. The human soul, touched at

its most sensitive spot, responds. The more that effective communication is drained of elements foreign to the work of art, elements that intervene between the emotion of the artist and the emotion of the spectator, the greater will be its precision and power.

The form of a thing is capable of awakening and producing emotions that become more intense as the form becomes less literal. The leaping horseman becomes more and more magical, increasingly representative of mythical thought, the further he departs from actual representation. He is not really himself, in the full meaning of the word, until the moment when he becomes pure energy, in his own space and time. Plastic form is an autonomous expression of space and time and has a constant tendency to the transcendental. When in *Backward Glances* Kandinsky looked back on the years 1910–1911 in order to assess the importance and meaning of the road he had traveled, he realized that "my unconscious quest for the disintegration of the painted object through its absorption by the painting had taught me the possibility of achieving a dissociation that would transcend the object itself on the canvas." In other words, the visionary creation of representational images in the 1905–1908 "Russian romantic" period, already described, was an attempt to supersede the object through a legendary transformation and dynamic transfiguration that would give it another interpretation, another bearing.

Although Kandinsky was always deeply attached to nature and received deep spiritual inspiration from it ever since his pre-1900 realist period, and still more during his Impressionist period from 1900 to 1905, he had never felt that material objects ought to be represented only according to their external appearance, their value as phenomena. The organization of plastic volumes and colors was independent of the subject shown in the picture and corresponded to an internal, emotive construction, one of feeling, which in turn responded to the vibrations of a sensibility able to extract, from the impact and reaction of exterior perception and internal vision, an autonomous and valid aesthetic, in which form tended to be no longer image but energy.

If the year 1910–1911 was the year of a triumphant breakthrough, that break had been anticipated by developments of the preceding years. Kandinsky's work is organically con-

MOSCOW LADY. 1912
STÄDTISCHE GALERIE, MUNICH

tinuous, and he proceeds by infiltrations rather than by rup-
tures; each infiltration of one stage by the next, with its chain

BLACK LINES. 1913
SOLOMON R. GUGGENHEIM MUSEUM, NEW YORK

of metamorphoses all implicit in one another, is the result of
continual ethical and aesthetic reflection and of constant en-

richment of the artist's means of expression. It is paralleled by deepening of his intellectual interests (a growing appreciation of the sciences) and of his spiritual ones (interest in new forms of thought, philosophy, religion, theosophy, and anthroposophy). Science and philosophy strangely affected Kandinsky's aesthetic and even his technical development. The new theories of astronomy, biology, and physics regarding the origin and structure of matter, the discovery that matter could be destroyed and transformed into energy, corresponded to the painter's discovery of the function of nature in art. Intellectually and spiritually, he was too close to all the great movements of thought for them not to make an impression on his work. Thus his art is not only one of the most marvelous aesthetic adventures of this and of all ages, but also reflects in plastic form many facets of modern anxiety in the face of the problems of existence and the hereafter.

Kandinsky's painting, as independent of philosophical problems as of nature, yet as responsive to the movement of ideas as to nature itself, mirrors the whole history of our times. An examination of his arrangement of form and color alone will not lead to a full understanding of his work; by revealing only a part, it would lead to misunderstanding. His work is above all an inward development. A consideration of the fifty years of the artist's activity clearly shows that material form is transformed into the spiritual through a succession of "enlightenments," which have for the artist—as is most obvious in his writings—the quality of revelation.

Few contemporary painters—perhaps none but Klee—have been as ready as Kandinsky to respond to strong spiritual demands and modify their aesthetic and technique in response to those demands. This was never through abrupt changes of mind or heart, but through continual pursuit of the principle of inner necessity, towards a constant objective that became steadily more insistent as it came closer. In Kandinsky's painting, aesthetic demands – the offspring of reflection and revelation – increasingly acquired the quality of religious dedication. At a time when people were much concerned with the social mission of art, it was natural for Kandinsky, too, to consider and analyze its social function before attaining what he called the "kingdom of the great spirituality."

How could this spirituality be attained? A study of the paintings produced during his ten-year "dramatic period" reveals that it was achieved principally by freeing the picture from subject matter, converting matter into energy, and keeping only the emotive form of the object. Everything that heretofore had weighed down art, that had made it heavy and material, limited to the world of appearances as perceived through the senses, now became wonderfully light and transparent. Impelled directly to the heart of an object, to the center where substance becomes idea, the artist avoided transitory appearances. He aspired to the eternal and, to realize this aspiration, he strove to reach elemental energy, which by endless changes continually renews itself.

It was in this period, and especially in 1911, that movement itself, and no longer merely the image of a moment of movement, or an allusion to movement, was first incorporated into a painting. This was one of Kandinsky's greatest artistic triumphs, and one that was to have great consequences. The painting is made up entirely of currents and cross-currents that retain the inward effervescence of the composition. A study of the dynamic modifications in such paintings as *Improvisation 6* (1910), *Improvisation 9* (1910), *Pastoral* (1911), the different versions of *St. George* (1911), *Romantic Landscape* (1911), *Composition V* (1911), *With the Black Arch* (1912), *Improvi-*

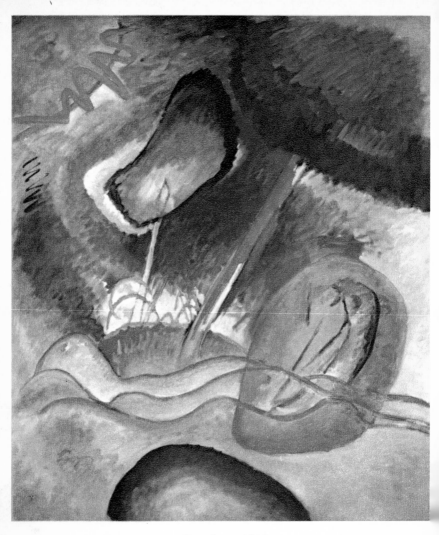

RED SPOT. 1913
STÄDTISCHE GALERIE, MUNICH

IMPROVISATION 31 (SEA BATTLE). 1913
COLLECTION DÜBI-MÜLLER, SOLOTHURN, SWITZERLAND

41

sation 30: Cannon (1913), the versions of *Deluge* (1912), *Painting with White Forms* (1913) and *Black Lines* (1913), to mention a few characteristic examples, shows that, in order to arrive at pure movement, the painter emptied the composition of all incidental narrative. The successive transformations of figures and objects (rider, landscape elements, ships) tend to convert them into pure vigor, into the absolute incarnation of a leap. Figures and objects dissolve in movement as though consumed by their own energy.

Certain pictures of this "dramatic period" preserve a representational or rather a figured substratum. For Kandinsky, the figure was not a hindrance to the liberation of spiritual content, any more than it was for Giotto, the icon painters of Novgorod, or the Byzantines. He was concerned only with pursuing the exploration of the reality that lies beyond perishable forms. Figurative form is transitional: the artist should regard it not as a barrier to reaching the spirit, but as a means of establishing contact with it. Thus there was nothing systematic or dogmatic in Kandinsky's elimination of the figure during this period. While from 1910 onwards he produced strictly abstract compositions, he also produced in 1910 and 1911 paintings in which representation, although certainly no longer the pretext for the picture, served as a base for experiments in formal and lyrical transformation. In this respect *Troïka* (1911), *Composition II* (1910), *Improvisation 20* (1911) are footnotes of considerable importance and interest in the story of his evolution towards a mystique of form. They display the dual aspects of the "dream landscapes" and the dramatic period, and the complex transition from one to the other.

There is never any interruption between one period and the next; the designations used to place a picture in its chronological sequence have only a relative value. Kandinsky's work

Painting on Light Ground. 1916
Collection Nina Kandinsky, Paris ▷

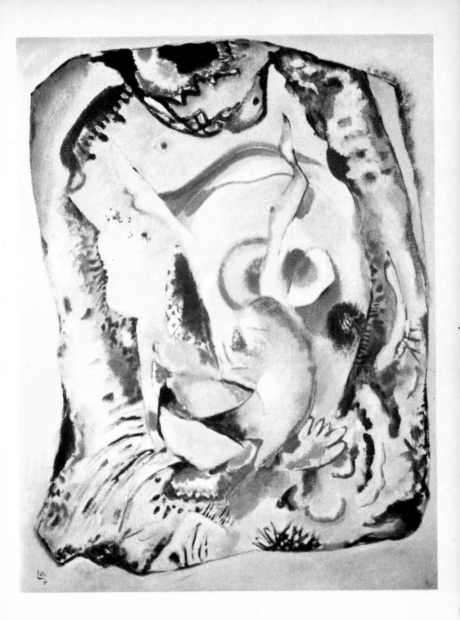

never stagnated in one formula or one manner; it was constantly changing. In the same way that each individual painting fascinates us because it is continually in process of self-creation, so the totality of his work in its rapid mutations – nine periods in less than fifty years – repeats the cycle of a living being, from its birth in matter to its release in spirit. Each painting is a transitional work that is always "becoming," and in which the future is inherent. The series of transitions from the "dream landscapes" to the "dramatic period," from the latter to the "architectural era" and thence to the "circles," and from them to the "romantic" compositions and the final "great synthesis" of the last ten years, resulted from an intense and uninterrupted inward struggle.

During the "dramatic period" movement, expressed as form, mingled the elements of space and of time appropriate to each painting. Each presented a new spiritual as well as a new plastic problem. In a flash of inspiration Kandinsky perceived the magical, mystical operation of creation, when he remarked, "To create a work is to create a world." The picture, *this* picture, is something new, something that did not exist before and which was lacking in the universe. The picture is an addition to the cosmos, and offers the spectator a means of entering into the cosmic totality through his understanding of this new entity. The picture also, said Kandinsky, has the capacity to activate the "psychic power of the individual," which in its turn should stimulate "the response of the human soul." It involves both body and soul, which when separated leave a mankind useless and divided. Kandinsky's ambition of achieving this harmonious relationship among the painter, the picture, the spectator, and the cosmos recalls Cézanne's more modestly phrased aspiration. For years Kandinsky's work progressed from explosion to explosion, each painting demanding and engendering a new technique, as is only natural, since each is a new living being that poses new problems. It was thus that, cataclysm by cataclysm, the earth evolved when its matter and form were elaborated according to a predestined internal formula, a governing design that is the result equally of spiritual and material necessity.

It was as though Kandinsky had unleashed natural forces like volcanoes, hurricanes, and tidal waves and disciplined them through his spiritual authority, taming and freezing them in their seething nostalgia for the infinite. Motion is hurled into tumultuous metamorphoses, forms swell and burst before liberating the energy that fills them. When the painter speaks of "the symphony known as the music of the spheres, which is the product of the chaotic uproar of the cosmic elements," he is referring to the convulsions of his own creation. He rejected pre-established harmony, and in an exalted mingling of anguish and joy, apparent in many paintings of his dramatic period, he strove to achieve a harmony of his own. Only this harmony seemed a living one to him, because it curtailed neither the life of created matter nor the life of the creative spirit. Kandinsky's initiation into the fascinating emotional power of non-representational expression did not mean a total break with nature; on the contrary, it meant that he penetrated into laboratories hidden in the depths of the unseen world, where he found new dimensions and discovered at the molten heart of primeval matter spiritual continents that we could not recognize if they were not matter.

The foundation of the Blue Rider resulted in the publication of a collective volume and in exhibitions in which foreign painters of very different tendencies (Braque, Rousseau, Delaunay) were invited to participate. The Blue Rider, one of the richest and most important movements in contemporary

VIEW FROM WINDOW OF APARTMENT IN MOSCOW. 1920
GEMEENTE MUSEUM, THE HAGUE

art, was distinguished not so much by an aesthetic of its own as by the common spirit shared by its principal originators. Kandinsky not only provided the title (the horseman that had reappeared constantly for ten years) but brought the force and power of his will and thought to the movement. His natural leadership showed itself in the artistic groups whose head he became, the Phalanx and the Neue Künstlervereinigung. Every activity of the Blue Rider was imbued with the dominating spiritual ideas that inspired his paintings and his book at that period. The history of the Blue Rider has often been told; it is not necessary to repeat it here, except to emphasize the leading role that Kandinsky played in it, and the vigor with which he impressed his ideas.

For the background, it is worth recalling how the movement came to be founded and named. Grohmann refers to the description Kandinsky gave in 1930 in *Das Kunstblatt* and draws attention to the significance that the painter attached to blue, "a typically celestial color that calls man to the infinite and awakens in him a nostalgic desire for purity and the supernatural." Thus it was not by chance that Marc and Kandinsky, seated one day on the terrace of the Café Sinseldorf, suddenly saw the image of the blue horseman as a firm bond between them, for both the color and the figure occupied an important place in their personal mythology.

The precepts that guided the members of the Blue Rider had strong similarities. Marc wrote, "How does one recognize an authentic work? As one recognizes everything that is authentic, by its inward life, which is the guarantee of its truth." He was here enunciating exactly the same principle as Macke, who said, "Every form of art is a manifestation of inner life"; and of Kandinsky himself, who said, "The beautiful is the product of inner necessity." The same idea found

RED OVAL. 1920
SOLOMON R. GUGGENHEIM MUSEUM, NEW YORK

its plastic formulation in an almost identical way in the
paintings of these three artists. Their parallel was the musician
Thomas von Hartmann, for whom "every means born of inner

BLACK SPOT. 1921
KUNSTHAUS, ZURICH

49

necessity is justified." Grohmann, who collated these quotations, suggests that their similarity indicates that the Blue Rider became the rallying cry and symbol of an artistic turning point that left a deep imprint upon modern aesthetic, primarily in music and painting, which were closely associated by their common ideal.

Kandinsky's art developed in the direction of lyrical enthusiasm, in which form and color were increasingly freed from any connection whatsoever with nature. Movement, which is the inward dynamism of form, was also freed from ties with narrative content and naturalistic representation. It was now realized that the painting could no longer represent anything but itself, its own intimate, pathetic, poetic content. Abstraction, as it now began to be called, was thus perfectly justified. Kandinsky was at this point of his development when, in 1914, the war necessitated his return to Russia, the source of his great colorist experiences; he was still passionately devoted to his native land, and he remained so strongly influenced by it that – he himself assures us – his "personal Russia" went with him to Munich and continued to influence his art, and particularly his sense of color.

During the years that he spent in Russia until his return to Germany in 1921, he found himself involved in political affairs and social upheavals; he was required for various posts, teaching art at the Academy, founding and reorganizing museums. He gave himself to these tasks, which interested him and satisfied his desire for community service, with the enthusiasm and devotion that he brought to all his activities, artistic or otherwise; but he found himself so engrossed in affairs that his output of painting was reduced. There are no pictures in the catalogue dating from 1915 or 1918, an exceptional omission in the life of an artist whose creative power continually developed with a rhythm that was seldom broken. It is difficult to give any estimate of the paintings executed in Russia, since they are mostly in Russian museums and not always accessible. Russia was being transformed both politically and aesthetically; it became less and less like the legendary fairyland of his youth. He himself had abandoned the romanticism that had formerly inspired him and that still appeared in some of the canvases of the Blue Rider period. He thus approached the new Russia, a product of war and revolution, with a fresh eye and a different sensibility. His teaching and museum activities also turned his mind towards entirely new interests. A profound transformation had taken place in Russia, where Constructivism now reigned supreme. Tatlin, Malevich, Gabo, Pevsner, and Lissitzky were working in a strictly geometrical abstract style that had no affinities with Kandinsky's aesthetic. Kandinsky probably taught alongside them at the art school, but as Grohmann states, "he was not especially interested in their work ... It is noteworthy that the Constructivists, in Russia down to 1921 and in Germany after 1921, had no close ties with Kandinsky, and tended to regard him as an opponent. He went his own way. He was very definitely attracted to Klee, just as Klee was to him, and although the differences between the two are very great, Kandinsky had much closer affinities with Klee than with the Constructivists, or than with the partisans of De Stijl, whose painting was similarly oriented."

Had the Russian landscape completely ceased to inspire Kandinsky's art, now that it had become abstract? It is difficult to say; impressions are no longer transmitted only through poetic emotion, but by an exceptionally powerful dramatic feeling, which is expressed in the works of the Moscow period with an unusual and striking organic intensity. His paintings

THROUGH-GOING LINE. 1923
PRIVATE COLLECTION, PARIS

present tornadoes whirling in space with elemental fury, forces
that probe the foundations of nature, the birth of living beings
as they struggle laboriously, painfully, to take shape and work
out a way of existence in a cataclysmic universe. They illustrate the conflict of currents of energy that collide, intersect,
or combine in an even more dramatic spirit than that which
animated the preceding period.

If one takes as examples of this new Russian period *Overcast*
(1917), *Two Ovals* (1919), *Variegated Circle* (1921) or *White
Background* (1920), one is overwhelmed by the violence of

INTIMATE COMMUNICATION. 1925
PRIVATE COLLECTION, PARIS

53

the cosmic upheavals that seem to have been captured in these paintings. Abstraction and the abolition of all remnants of natural form have unleashed a power of representing the invisible that is carried as far as it will go. This is not so evident in *Circles Within Black* (1921) or *Blue Segment* (1921), where the presence of a few almost geometrical forms is reassuring. But in the strange "agonistic" compositions, where all the forces of nature are hurled against one another in a drama that is no longer scaled to man but to the universe, the spectator is present at the convulsions of a cosmos in process of creation. *Entrance* (1917), *Clarity* and *Twilight* of the same year, *Painting with Two Red Spots* and *Painting on Light Ground* (1916) are related to the abstractions of the Munich period but show a development towards an increasingly dominant and sometimes oppressive cosmic feeling. It is as though Spirit had given way to Matter.

CREATION AND TEACHING

The period that began in 1921 and was to extend over twelve years was distinguished by intense teaching activity, simultaneous with creative expressions that were highly varied both in their forms and in the ideas that inspired them. The Bauhaus of Weimar and Dessau, which had played a highly important role in the evolution of modern art, was assured of a master of exceptional worth when Kandinsky was installed. For the painter himself, the appointment provided an outlet for his outstanding teaching ability. Although at Munich he had occasionally taught painting in his own studio, at the Bauhaus he found himself in a highly organized environment, where under Gropius' direction instruction in the plastic and the

54

applied arts was carried on simultaneously. It was Gropius' clearly visualized and energetically expressed desire to effect a fusion between the schools of the so-called fine arts and the decorative arts. Artists and craftsmen were thus required to work side by side. All the painters who taught at the Bauhaus –Klee, Feininger, and above all Kandinsky–have spoken of the advantages that they derived from the quasi-industrial experience acquired through contact with workshops of ceramics, weaving, cabinet-making, and metalwork.

Walter Gropius regretted that artists and craftsmen normally work separately and without intercommunication, thus losing the advantages that would spring from productive collaboration; and so he organized at Weimar, and later moved to Dessau, the vast establishment known as Bauhaus. The name itself indicated that it was in actuality a workshop, a sort of construction site, in which ideas, techniques, projects and the means of their realization, in every field of artistic activity from architecture to ballet, were worked out jointly.

The history of the Bauhaus from its establishment in 1919 to its disbanding in 1933 is an account of how the second quarter of this century became one of the most remarkable and productive periods in German art. Through its spirit an achievements, the Bauhaus gave a new direction to contemporary aesthetics, and one still sees the influence of its artistic ethic with its strong emphasis on functionalism. Gropius' desire for unity inspired him to found this melting pot, where personalities as different as those of Schlemmer, Moholy-Nagy, and Muche were associated in a collective work comparable to the stone-yards of the Middle Ages in which masons and artists had worked side by side. It was first necessary in Gropius' scheme to abolish the class solidarity of guilds of artisans, and to attract artists to the manual work of iron forging and glass blowing. It was a social ideal, a dream of a "new building of the future ... crystalline emblem of the new faith in the future," to be built by millions of workers and artists who would realize their common interest in a new concept of construction. "Our ultimate goal," said Gropius, "which is still far off, is the unified work of art, the 'great work' in which no distinction between monumental and decorative art will remain."

In the text Kandinsky wrote for the collective work entitled *Das Staatliche Bauhaus in Weimar,* published in 1923, he expressed total adherence to Gropius' program. Under the heading, "Fundamental Elements of Form," Kandinsky indicated the main, essentially technical, lines that his instruction would follow. His synopsis of the course in handling color also reveals the same characteristics of effective, practical simplicity. This was very far from the messianic concept of painting that had inspired *On the Spiritual in Art;* the problems of form now took first place (not, however, without allusion being made to their spiritual implications), as can also be seen in the volume *Point and Line to Plane,* published in 1926. The very title of this theoretical didactic treatise shows how seriously the painter took his role of professor and the interest he took in the value of his instruction. In his course, for example, he would demonstrate the different ways of handling a still life or even a nude – remarkable for an artist whose own work was already completely abstract.

Kandinsky had been associated previously with collective efforts when he was working with the Phalanx and the Neue Künstlervereinigung, and even to a certain extent with The Blue Rider. Things were very different at the Bauhaus, where the atmosphere was that of a lay monastery, and where he experienced the sometimes oppressive demands of communal living. But the close contact with the great artists who, like him, lived at the Bauhaus, more than compensated him. As Mies van der Rohe puts it, Kandinsky made the Bauhaus idea "his," and his adoption of its message appears in his words to Grohmann: "In addition to synthetic collaboration, I expect from each art a further powerful, entirely new inner development, a deep penetration, liberated from all external purposes, into the core of the human spirit, which only there begins to touch the world spirit." Elsewhere he said, "We work under the banner of synthesis." The attraction that this banner held for the artist is obvious. His every effort, from the beginning of his life as a painter, had been directed towards realizing the synthesis of elements that were antagonistic or at least scattered, and his last works, those of the Parisian period from 1933 to 1944, were concerned with the great synthesis.

If one tries to ascertain what gifts Kandinsky brought to the Bauhaus, and what benefits he received in exchange, one finds that the deepening of his personality and the broadening of his technique were the most important results of those years, while the enrichment of his inner self had as its counterpart an ability to give of himself more openly and generously. Grohmann writes: "His closest contacts were with Klee, who used the opportunity to experiment just as enthusiastically as Kandinsky, stimulated by intelligent experiments made in the preliminary course by Ittens, and later by Albers and Moholy-Nagy, who worked with the most varied materials and formal requirements. They were also inspired by the works made by both teachers and students (masters and apprentices) in the various classes. They were interested in Hirschfeld-Mack's investigations of color and light, in the techniques of weaving, in Oskar Schlemmer's stage experiments and *Triadic Ballet*, and not least in the study of spatial problems by architects." Kandin-

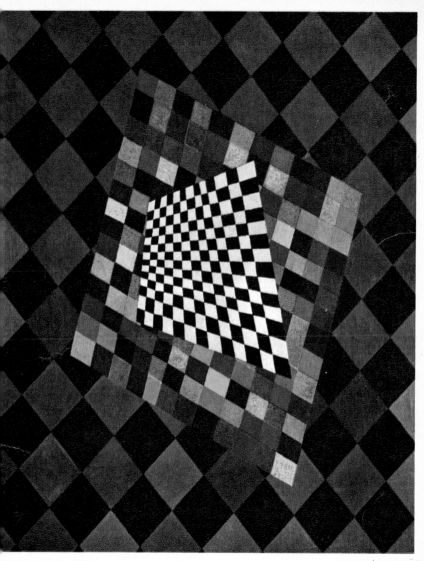

SQUARE. 1927
COLLECTION AIMÉ MAEGHT, PARIS

59

sky's interest in the theater led him to write some plays that were to be produced with associated music and light; this answered his desire for a complete work of art, a *Gesamtkunst-werk*, an old Romantic ideal whose realization was made possible by the very nature of the Bauhaus. At the Bauhaus, he found himself in continual contact with the concrete — concrete in the work of the studios, in the dominating ideas of the group, and in the manual work that continually opened new horizons.

Although Kandinsky's paintings of these ten years were not, strictly speaking, directly inspired by the program and activities of the Bauhaus, they show strong affinities with them that should not be misunderstood. The treatise *Point and Line to Plane*, while not intended either as a guide or a commentary, is necessary as an aid to understanding and seeing these works in all their unity. The basic graphic elements now provided the best means of discovering through theory another pathway to the spiritual; one can even discern in this treatise a sort of "point mystique," whose application is demonstrated in Kandinsky's paintings, especially those of the "circle" period. Yet far from removing the line from nature, Kandinsky, by following its behavior in living organic forms like crystals, emphasized the analogies between intellectual constructions and biological processes. The movement of the hand that draws a circle or a square, or that follows the trajectory of a point to create a form on a surface, is not just a personal or abstract activity: the forces of nature participate and express themselves through it. The symbolism of form is itself a reflection of these forces in motion, and its meaning is both physical and mental.

This treatise becomes of fundamental importance when one realizes that it should not be read simply as an instructional text designed for students, but as a testament of formal principles that are equally recognizable in Kandinsky's paintings. A study of the paintings of the Weimar period together with the illustrations for his book *Point and Line to Plane* reveals the same aesthetic preoccupations respecting the plastic organization of form, starting from first premises that seem very elementary but are in reality extremely complex. The woodcuts entitled *Kleine Welten (Little Worlds)* that accompany the poems in *Klänge (Reverberations)* are likewise in their own way illustrations to this little educational booklet, comparable from this point of view to the *Pedagogical Sketchbooks* of Klee, which were also produced at the Bauhaus, for the Bauhaus, and in the Bauhaus spirit.

Grohmann has noted that, if the Blue Rider contained elements of Romanticism, the Bauhaus period may be called classical; but it was a classicism in constant progress, in incessant evolution, increasingly directed towards openness. Kandinsky's character was endowed with two aspects, the romantic and the classical, and his greatness lies in his ability to make use of each in the equilibrium he established between their antitheses, with the truly Goethe-like alternations of systole and diastole that can be observed in him: expansion towards the world outside himself, and a more intense concentration on the inmost depths of his own personality. The variety of alternations is apparent in the diversity of his pictorial ideas (in the same sense as one speaks of "musical ideas") in the three successive periods between 1920 and 1933. But no more than in preceding years do these chronological periods signify that the components of his art are separated by watertight bulkheads. The development of a painter's work is like an organic phenomenon, especially with Kandinsky, where everything evolves in an uninterrupted sequence; divisions into periods are neces-

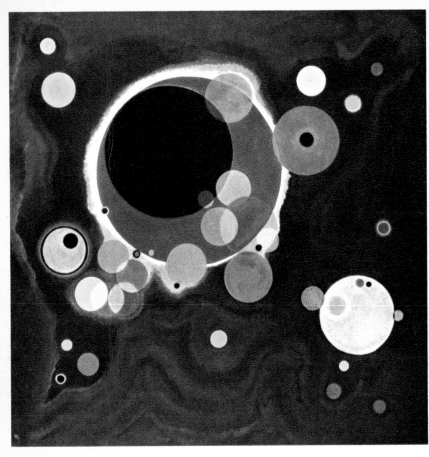

SEVERAL CIRCLES. 1926
SOLOMON R. GUGGENHEIM MUSEUM, NEW YORK

sary only for the purposes of historic classification and definition. Kandinsky's paintings display the characteristics of bio-

ON POINTS. 1928
COLLECTION NINA KANDINSKY, PARIS

logical growth and bloom like living beings: this ensures that
they are connected with one another by an unbroken line; at

most there is a knot marking a pause, a change of direction or a turning point. His two major writings, *On the Spiritual in Art* (1911) and *Point and Line to Plane* (1926), are signposts along the road, indicating his most important and characteristic tendencies. With them should be considered the texts written in defence of abstract art, published in 1931 in *Cahiers d'Art*. They also have the value of testaments, vindicating the message of the artist as man, as painter and as philosopher.

The works that were painted in the period beginning with his return from Russia – when he settled in Berlin, and later moved to the Bauhaus – and ending with his departure for Paris, fall into three groups: "architectural" (1920–1924), "circles" (1925–1927), and "the romanticism of concrete art" (1927–1933). Though the paintings themselves need no commentary, since each picture in itself is sufficient to communicate directly to the spectator everything that the latter is capable of comprehending, the terms designating the periods demand some clarification.

The architectural period is also sometimes called, in Kandinsky's own words, his "cold" period, but in order to avoid grave misunderstanding, it is necessary to explain what he meant. These paintings are "cold" only when contrasted with the romantic ardor of the preceding period, which Grohmann calls "the period of genius." By this he did not mean that Kandinsky manifested more genius then than in other periods of his life, but rather that the imminence and effusion of genius as such, in its frenetic abundance and its warmth of color, was evidence of a lyricism, fairly close in sentiment if not in means of expression, to the dream landscapes of 1908–1910. Whether one calls it the "dramatic" period or the "period of genius," the decade of 1910–1919 still contained a romanticism to which Kandinsky's teaching activity and still more the activity of the Bauhaus put an end, for the moment at least. It was to reappear in a different form at the end of his stay in Dessau, whither Kandinsky had followed the Bauhaus when political events obliged this organization to leave Weimar.

To characterize the paintings from 1921 to 1925, I prefer to use the word "remote" rather than the ambiguous "cold." Remote actually means the accentuation of objectivity; the object becomes more detached from the artist and receives an autonomous vitality that is more independent of its creator; it establishes a certain order of laws and principles to which it conforms. Geometrical forms introduced an austerity unknown in the artist's work up to then. The treatise on point and line did not inspire his painting, but rather reflected its demands and aspirations. The intellectual phenomenon was superimposed on the spiritual, without substituting for it completely; the cold light of intelligence cooled the scalding anxiety and passion that had raised the "temperature" of the earlier pictures.

One might select as typical of this moment *Variegated Circle* (1921), *Circles Within Black* (1921), *On White* (1923), *One Center* (1924), *Calm Tension* (1924), *Black Relation* (1924), *Small Dream in Red* (1925), *Double Ascension* (1925), *Yellow-Red-Blue* (1925), *Composition VIII* (1923), *Black Accompaniment* (1924), all very indicative of the geometrization of form and the cooling of color. In their tendency towards an abstraction that was stylistic rather than lyrical, there can be discerned a vague and distant echo of the De Stijl group. Although much cooler, Kandinsky's use of color remains extremely refined, sometimes reducing color to an almost imperceptible fine powder, as though to overcome the density of a medium that might make his form opaque and heavy. These paintings are infinitely "light": objects, most often enclosed in

GREEN DEGREES. 1929
PRIVATE COLLECTION, PARIS

geometrical forms, float in an environment created in a void, on very luminous, light colored backgrounds. An extraordinary transparency and brilliance make the paint substance almost impalpable; the architecture of the composition is made up of forms of surprising elasticity that bound into space and float with the same sprightliness as that of a living organism that has eliminated the feeling of weight.

Sometimes in this aerial ballet of translucent balls and crystalline arrows, the spectator is surprised to find fragments of natural objects such as boats, just recognizable, but their appearance at all is puzzling. In combination with this delicate paint medium, this unequivocal, unambiguous simplification of shape, this clearly defined geometry, all this might appear haphazard in the work of any other painter, but Kandinsky's work does not give this impression; the very notion of fortuity is quite irreconcilable with his ever-present sense of inner necessity. In this case, inner necessity is defined by the very word "architecture." The structures presented are not merely capricious compositions of forms; their relationship is ordered according to natural law, as inevitable as the law that governs physical bodies. They play freely in space with purified, clarified movements, in which there is no longer any trace of the organic, impetuous rhythms of the Blue Rider and the "genius" periods. It could be said that the object's own inner spirit had imposed itself on that of the artist, or at least had worked together and actively co-operated with him, as was to happen in the period of the great synthesis.

Amongst the geometrical forms, through which there still flowed the rhythms molded by flesh and soil of the abstract pictures of the preceding years, the circle already began to assume the symbolic and plastic preponderance that it had in Kandinsky's soul, so revealing of the spirit of his painting. Geometrical forms have their own vitality and personality, and they are quite capable of pathos. This can be seen in *Black*

RADIATING LINES. 1927

ANGULAR LINE. 1930
NATIONAL GALLERY OF MODERN ART, ROME

69

Relation, for example, where structural conflict hints at spiritual strife between the group of angular figures and the commanding, proud solitude of the enormous, dark, menacing circle. Although it dates from the "architectural" period, because of its meaning this picture can be said in some respects to inaugurate the "circle" period. It is an excellent illustration of one extremely important aspect of Kandinsky's thought, mythological rather than symbolic, for the myth is itself the living thing for which the symbol serves as a token.

The preponderance of circles in the architectural period, and still more between 1925 and 1927, corresponded to some inner necessity. What this was, Kandinsky has explained in his highly revealing letters written to Will Grohmann, and in the text published by Plaut in 1929 following his investigation of the artist's psychology. "If I make such frequent, vehement use of the circle in recent years, the reason (or cause) for this is not the geometric form of the circle, or its geometric properties, but my strong feeling for the inner force of the circle and its countless variations; I love the circle today as I formerly loved the horse, for instance—perhaps even more, since I find more inner potentialities in the circle, which is why it has taken the horse's place."

The inner potentialities are those that connect the plastic with the spiritual and make the circle, even in its superficial aspect, an allusion to the absolute and the transcendental. Kandinsky's paintings of the Bauhaus period, dominated by geometrical forms, can be read as arrangements of spatial structures, in which the triangle, the rectangle, and the circle combine and oppose their forces. One can also notice how in a painting like *Yellow-Red-Blue,* for example, or *Black Accompaniment,* a balance of forces is established between closed and open forms, forms in contraction and those in expansion.

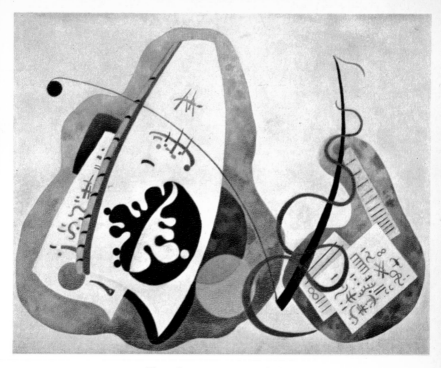

TWO SURROUNDINGS. 1934
STEDELIJK MUSEUM, AMSTERDAM

In them one can catch the play of a certain cosmic energy that, under the mask of a caprice of color, delineates the essential features of universal energy that is translated, plastically speaking, into the simplest and the most generally descriptive symbols.

It is a sort of code, to which the painter offers the key – at least to the interpretation of the circle, when in a letter to Grohmann (October 12, 1930), he offers the following striking definition. The circle is "the most modest form, but asserts itself unconditionally, a precise but inexhaustible variable, simultaneously stable and unstable, simultaneously loud and soft, a single tension that carries countless tensions within it." On the level of pure form, where the formal verges on the spiritual, "the circle is the synthesis of the greatest oppositions. It combines the concentric and the eccentric in a single form, and in balance. Of the three primary forms (triangle, square, circle), it points most clearly to the fourth dimension." These words should not be construed as an indication of an esoteric circle cult. They show that Kandinsky was investigating simultaneously the supernatural and natural, the synthetic and amalgamating properties of the circle. It was by painting circles, not by constructing an hermetic scientific theory, that Kandinsky discovered, through and beyond its variations, the powerful significance of its primary structure, the center from which radiated the energy that suffused the picture in subtly contrasted waves.

"The circle ... is a link with the cosmic. But I use it above all formally." All Kandinsky's intellectual and artistic pronouncements are summed up in these few words. Before anything else, the circle is a form, endowed with formal properties, but it is also through its form that it develops its enormous possibilities. When paintings such as *Chat* (1926), *Several Circles* (1926), *Quiet* (1926), *Black Increasing* (1927), *Closely Surrounded* (1926), *Dark Impulse* (1926), *Simple* (1927) are analyzed, a sort of planetary consciousness can be observed in the action of spheres revolving in space. I say spheres because, although the painter never attempts three-dimensional illusionism, he achieves the representation of suggested volume by the chromatic intensity of the surrounding forms and the reference to time that is implicit in the movement of the planets.

Perhaps it may not be paradoxical to suggest that in paintings such as these, Kandinsky achieves the third dimension by striving for the fourth. The constellations that travel their courses in a space itself crisscrossed by violent currents, comparable to cosmic rays, possess the mysterious vitality of organic forms. In contrast to the strict laws of the Dutch members of De Stijl, who were also mystics in their way, the laws that govern Kandinsky's universe retain the vibrant feeling of life evolving across infinite space; his universe is not allegorical but real, plastic and formal – form being understood as a stage towards the perception of that which is no longer form. Possibly the knowledge that Kandinsky had of the thought and philosophy of the East, already noted in *On the Spiritual in Art,* in which he outlined a theosophy which is a synthesis of Asia and Europe, inclined him towards the Chinese and Indian doctrines that postulate a mysterious science of forms comparable to the science of numbers.

Kandinsky, always preoccupied with the numerous implications of the romantic idea, finally began to speak of the "romanticism of the circle." The very notion of indefinable space is a romantic concept, just as is the conviction that there are phenomena that escape analysis; such ideas were dear to the painter. He broke loose from the circles when the period of "the romanticism of concrete art" began. This terminology demands some commentary and explanation; the word "concrete," like the word "abstract," is subject to contradictory interpretations. When trying to define this new method of creating, which drew forms from the absolute of his invention instead of borrowing them from nature's formal vocabulary, he needed an adjective to describe it exactly. Abstract and concrete, antonyms in everyday language, are here made applicable to the same idea: that of non-representational art. It

74   MOVEMENT. 1935
COLLECTION NINA KANDINSKY, PARIS

LIGHT CONSTRUCTION. 1940
COLLECTION HERMANN RUPF, BERN

75

would seem that, in this sense, abstract and concrete had the same meaning for Kandinsky. Non-representational forms were absolutely concrete – pure concrete, while at the same time they were the result of a process of abstraction that consisted of eliminating the natural forms from which, for thousands of years, artists had traditionally borrowed their formal repertory.

Kandinsky has taken his position in the debate and written his interpretation of abstract and concrete in unequivocal terms. The joint experiments of artists and craftsmen at the Bauhaus reinforced his feeling for the material; the sensory, and especially tactile, contact with the substance of an object developed in him a lasting appreciation of the concrete. If the Bauhaus was an idea, it was a factory of forms much more than a laboratory of ideas, or rather, no idea was conceived there which was not expressed in an object. This was the great source of its strength, and the secret of the productivity of Gropius' idea. There was never the slightest tendency towards intellectualism for its own sake. All thought was matter, all matter thought. The distance between the artistic object and the work of art diminished, so that any distinction between them became more difficult, and aesthetic phenomena were driven into "concretization" with ever-increasing force. If abstract art is intellectual, Kandinsky's art is firmly and strongly concrete, for he goes beyond intellectualism in every dimension: on the one hand, in the direction of a more lively, more acute and richer sensuousness, and on the other hand towards a spirituality that masks his means and enlarges his aspirations. He does not orientate his art towards a new unreality; on the contrary, he creates reality, a concrete reality. This is the derivation of the term "romanticism of concrete art," under which are grouped the paintings executed between 1927 and his leaving the Bauhaus.

Kandinsky's inventiveness, which is one of the greatest merits of his prolific imagination, is demonstrated in the creation of new worlds emanating from one another in perpetual mutations. Grohmann puts it perfectly when he says, "These qualities and tensions are infinite in number. It is the sum total of the various relationships among line, plane, rhythm, melody, both at the formal and the spiritual or psychological level. More and more the paintings become phenomena that elude simple analysis: words cannot do justice to the multidimensional character of so free a conception." There are numerous pictures among the works of this period in which this multidimensional quality is displayed: *Points in Arc* (1927), *Radiating Lines* (1927), *Lyrical Oval* (1928), *On Points* (1928), *Picture Within Picture* (1929), *Stubborn* (1929). In certain pictures, marine themes—rolling waves, sails, masts, and hulls—appear and disappear, taking on geometrical forms or becoming animated, sometimes appearing to play hide-and-seek with the spectator. There are certain pictures suggesting seascapes that have exploded, and whose fragments have been projected into space and remain suspended in the midst of a neutral atmosphere, which is no longer that of either an abstract painting or a representational one. It is interesting to speculate on the source of this predilection, which led Kandinsky to connect remembered objects with imagined ones, and to treat forms recalling objective reality as purely plastic elements.

This process had nothing to do with the stylization of the Cubists or their fragmentary reconstructions. It had the delicacy and subtlety of a game of analogies; Kandinsky's forms are associations of images, in the sense that one speaks of an association of ideas. They are neither hieroglyphs, nor signs, but musical "cadences" or projections of analogous forms, although always, in Grohmann's phrase, "likeness of a higher

78
LIGHT TENSION. 1935
COLLECTION HERMANN RUPF, BERN

order." It would be ridiculous to see in all this a possible return to the representational; rather, the choice of invented forms is so free that it can admit even those with some resemblance to natural forms. Kandinsky's independence of nature stands out even more emphatically through his masterly juggling with what could be found in nature. He is not trying to mislead the spectator, nor to anger him, nor to reassure him by offering him something he has seen before; the spirit of the picture determines the choice of the structures and their arrangement. All else is incidental and worth mentioning only as a curiosity.

Ludwig Grote once wrote, "Kandinsky's biography is a succession of revelations that color presented to him." In the series of paintings between 1927 and 1933 in which the so-called romanticism of concrete art developed, the artist received the revelation of a new, highly refined chromatic order, very certain of its aims and methods. The powerful expansion of dramatic color that he had sought uninterruptedly for thirty years now reappeared in unexpected guise, renewed and enriched by the aesthetic and technical experience of the Bauhaus. *Evasion* (1931), *Development in Brown* (1933), *On a Blue Background* (1930) and *From-To* (1930) — whose title is only puzzling to those who are not familiar with the painter's spiritual pronouncements — move us by a sense of mystery rather different from that previously displayed; theirs is a musical mystery with rich overtones. Often troubled by the Kierkegaardian alternative of "Either–Or," Kandinsky ordered his work like a balancing and conflict of forces which, though not opposed, were capable of antagonism because of their very parallelism.

At the end of the Bauhaus period, when the closing of this amazing workshop of modern art scattered its members throughout every country in which free and independent artistic creativity was still possible, new roads opened to Kan-

dinsky, where all his experiments and discoveries of the previous years seemed to converge. *Evasion* and *Development in Brown* are the most eloquent witnesses of a different manner of treating color so that it seemed to speak another language, leading the artist into new spatial explorations. From the threshold of an unknown world that he had not yet investigated, Kandinsky advanced into a universe that was in marked contrast to everything already familiar to him and that demanded from his imagination the creation of new living forms.

THE GREAT SYNTHESIS

What is the meaning of the term "great synthesis," which is currently used to designate the period of Kandinsky's work throughout the last ten years of his life which he spent in Paris? In what respect does his output during this extraordinarily productive decade, completely fresh in its spirit and forms, represent a more accomplished, more definitive synthesis than the paintings of the preceding years? For half a century, Kandinsky had been inspired by his desire for a synthesis—a synthesis of his philosophical thought, his dramatic sentiment, his joy in color and his technical means of expression. This aspiration had sent him exploring paths which, while they seemed to spread out like a fan, were secretly converging towards a single point. Just before achieving this synthesis, Kandinsky's art passed through many stages, while at the same time he returned to the "Russian colors" of the beginning of his career as a painter. He was strongly influenced by Asiatic memories, probably the product of some atavistic resurgence, and showed a joyful baroque exuberance and an indefatigable desire to create forms that are living beings although bearing no ostensible relation to nature. During these ten years in which Kandinsky's aesthetic, as revealed in his paintings, broadened considerably, he set down in a number of important writings his ideas about the process of abstraction (or concretization, according to the vocabulary employed). His writings must be studied together with his paintings if either is to be understood. He also emerged as a prolific creator of original myths, inventing both their elements and their episodes.

Sometimes his style in his last paintings disconcerts those who do not understand the extent to which these works represent a summation of all his prior achievements. From 1933, when he settled in Paris, until his death in 1944, Kandinsky, in a style neither willful nor esoteric, propagated a strange multitude of creatures of striking reality, although they bear no resemblance to the reality that we know, apart from an indefatigable nervous energy that has been compared with the activity of the minute organisms revealed under a microscope.

These picturesque, capricious sprites, each created out of nothing, yet strikingly believable and effective, are movement clothed in form and color. So that the freedom of these movements may remain intact, the paint becomes extraordinarily light, glossy and brilliant; shadows and darkness are eliminated, and the palette displays its full chromatic range in weightless clarity. There is no more opacity and no more gravity in this universe, which seems peopled with extraordinarily personal, individualized, vibrating crystals, almost inspired in their respective peculiarities.

A superficial observer who had only a vague knowledge of the life to be seen through a microscope might be tempted to say that the painter had acquired an interest in natural science and become fascinated with infusoria or microbes, studying them to discover laws of life other than those that he had already examined. But this was not so. Far from inclining towards shapes not normally visible to the naked eye, Kandinsky was investigating another domain: that of plausible reality – of "potential figuration," as Grohmann puts it, or of what might be called "possible worlds," to use a phrase of Klee's that might be applied to the worlds of Miró and Tanguy as well as to that of Kandinsky in his last years.

The term "possible worlds" postulates the existence, in dimensions with which we are unfamiliar and governed by coordinates of time and space other than ours, of forms of life that our senses and mind cannot reveal to us because they lie beyond our perceptive faculties. Each of Kandinsky's paintings is the image of a world without antecedent, unexpected because it is the product of combinations never employed before. An invented world can be as "real" as the familiar world of natural forms, and it is possible to formulate its physical laws, describe its physiology and relate its history. This is neither impossible nor improbable; our age is more interested in the creation of possible worlds than in stale repetitions of a world aready too well known. Kandinsky's poetic gift, the faculty that made him invoke a new myth to support a new painting, helped him to achieve his liberation from nature by inventing another nature – valid for him and true to itself, but sometimes difficult for us to understand because it is a phenomenon as astonishing as it would be if a scientist were to see completely unknown beings spring from a chemical substance that he had placed under his microscope.

I stress the word "beings": the figures of Kandinsky's last period are beings, and not just the forms of beings. They are not the images of things, but the things themselves, which spring to life from the moment they are painted as though in response to a magical incantation; they are captive on the canvas, but live out their own existence there. One of the most striking characteristics of the period from 1910 to the present day is that Surrealism and abstraction have in common their invention of new beings; they ceaselessly elaborate a fantastic universe, drawn out of the void by the artist, yet intensely convincing. With the Surrealists, these objects still keep some resemblance to ordinary nature; but Klee, Miró, Tanguy, and Kandinsky seem to have discovered the keys to a domain that is not simply unexpected or incongruous, but incommensurate with the world we know and without any resemblance to it.

The fact that the paintings of Kandinsky's Parisian period all belong to this other realm of existence gives them a certain unity. But in their composition, their structure, and the manner in which the figures are related to one another and communicate with each other, one can distinguish three categories. These may be designated as compartmented paintings; those in which the autonomy of individual forms establishes the relation of the shapes in an "environment"; and lastly, those in which the elements group themselves according to additive or clustering principles of composition. Some monumental, haunting paintings of the very last years, 1943 and 1944, clothed in a sort of menacing, funereal richness, may be left for separate consideration because of their extreme singularity.

Among the compartmented paintings, the most characteristic examples of this mode of composition, *Sweet Trifles* (1937), *Each for Itself* (1934), *Various Parts* (1940), *Division-Unity* (1934), *Ensemble* (1940), well represent the curious humor that houses each of the forms, or beings, in an individual dwelling, as though to express its personality better, just as the different cages of a zoölogical garden separate animals of different species. Thus divorced from all structural context, from all synthetic composition, the shapes that make up the painting are

84

defined by their very isolation; their immobility within their individually allotted frames has the effect of powerfully concentrating an inward, vital energy that cannot be expended outwards. The compartmentation is not always as accentuated, regular and symmetrical as in the ironically chequered *Sweet Trifles*; there is more flexibility, more variety, and suggestion of currents of life circulating from box to box in *Each for Itself*, where the living cells thrust pseudopods towards their neighboring cells, thus combining a movement to the exterior with the seething life at the inmost core of its being.

Some of these compartmented pictures carry titles that precisely define the number of compartments: *Thirty* (1937), *Fifteen* (1938), *Seven* (1943); but there is a clearly noticeable difference among the three pictures. If the divisions of the first two are strictly numerical, the seven compartments of the third – closest to the artist's death – can scarcely retain their inmates. These forms, extraordinarily active forces that seem to move and change before our eyes, recall the seven demons of Slavonic mythology. Their movement, tinged with a certain aggressive energy, threatens to burst the cell walls: one believes that nothing could resist the fury of their will to live, the powerful driving force that inspires them. It is then that one realizes the extent to which the creator may eventually be controlled and possessed by his creations. They can become independent of him and inaugurate generations of strange, unprecedented organisms, destined to undergo miraculous mutations whose full potentialities are already inherent in their germs.

Each of these compartmented paintings – like all Kandinsky's pictures – presents a different problem, so varied are their meanings and the means of expressing their significance. These restlessly moving, constantly changing forms cannot be compared to cryptographic symbols, because they are never stable and never repeated. Each is completely independent of the others and even seems to live in a personal world, a world that it does not share and cannot share with anything, for its absolute individuality prohibits any sense of communion. The dynamic potential of these beings is so strong that one can believe that it was necessary to isolate them in anti-osmotic cells, to avoid the explosions that their inward forces would release if they were to find themselves together. Sometimes, however—as in *Succession* (1935)—the forms are aligned in horizontal rows that recall musical staves, and are linked together in a continuous development that suggests a musical phrase, a song; they establish unifying harmonies among themselves in this linear sequence. Looking at this painting, one thinks of the reels of abstract film by Hans Richter or Viking Eggeling, but the plastic necessity that could make one form evolve out of another is not present; Kandinsky's little personages remain obstinately individualist and particular. Kandinsky has given two canvases the same title, *Division-Unity*. In the first of these, dated 1934, the forms are disposed among the fields of a diamond-shaped trelliswork. Nine years later, the same name was given to a work executed in a quite different spirit. The apposition of these two words is too unusual for there not to be some deep meaning behind it, a meaning which the later painting especially tempts us to decipher. The spectator is here confronted with the concept of analysis and synthesis on which Kandinsky reflected so much during his entire life. No antithesis is contained in this concept: on the contrary, the living thing, the living being, is at the same time both analytic and synthetic. Emphatically, the analysis of the constituent elements of each form and of the content of each element—in a process which could go on indefinitely—remains ultimately a constructive analysis, that is to say a synthesis, but a synthesis of the infinitely small contained within the infinitely large; if we postulate that this operation continues unceasingly, then . . .

Because each form obeys its individual and intimate organic laws, it remains absolutely unique in the universe Kandinsky created in his Parisian period, in which is unfolded the inventory of all possible configurations that the imagination can discover in the multiple and infinitely varied repertory of living beings. These entities also adapt themselves to a form of social life, moving in the midst of a crowd of other beings unlike themselves—for there are no others like them—thus posing a new problem, that of relationship, of mutual agreement. The strict autonomy of an individual form does not prevent it from diving and swimming in an environment where, together with other heterogeneous creatures, it adapts itself and works out rules for harmony.

The picture called *Relations* (1934) is very instructive. An indescribable agitation, far more disturbed than Brownian movement, fills a space which itself becomes alive through being traversed in every direction by bodies that, without failing to obey their own personal rhythms, which differ in speed, direction, and intensity, give birth to a constellation constructed and actuated according to harmonious relationships. There are no longer partitions between the waving, spiraling, wriggling creatures that fill the field of vision; their idiosyncrasies have lost none of their hostility, but they utilise their dynamic antagonisms to create a system of attraction and repulsion acceptable to each one.

In *Center with Accompaniment* (1937), *Reciprocal Accord* (1942), and *Two Surroundings* (1934), these societies of contrasting individuals are controlled by an extremely flexible musical unity. The reality and necessity of each individual now develops reciprocally with that of every other individual. All the systems of composing groups and movements are as individual and unlike each other as the individual forms themselves. They range from a degree of compartmentation *(Striped,* 1934) to the extreme freedom, the melodious, calm and happy concord, of *Tempered Elan* (1944), one of Kandinsky's finest canvases and the most typical of the direction he was following at the time of his death. *Reciprocal Accord,* with its metrical arrangement of light colors dramatically contrasted with tragic black streaks, is one of the best examples of these "societies of objects" in which the society has its own vitality, its own powerful and vigorous individuality, equal to that of the objects which are mutually associated with it.

The principles according to which the objects are added and gathered together in the paintings where construction by means of groupings dominates, *Movement I* (1935), *Environment* (1936), *Composition IX* (1936), *Animated Stability* (1937), render the cell walls invisible and transform them, too, into plastic, moving, changing bodies capable of metamorphoses. Freedom of association, as sovereign as the freedom to exist and establish one's own personal identity, has been given to the inhabitants of this Kandinsky world. His art became free and ever more imbued with mobility, and grew still closer to life, because he created life rather than merely representing it. In his last, Parisian period, the painter's art completed the succession of metamorphoses that he had initiated when he renounced themes taken from nature. Transformations in color developed side by side with those in form, showing the same tendencies and closely linked in time. A limpid, pure, cold, generally extremely transparent color scheme was appropriate for the world of vibrating bodies, which had no relationship to things existing in nature and were invented without reference to the natural world. Kandinsky always liked glossy paint, but in his last years this sheen became comparable to the brilliance of a crystal. Perhaps the painter was seeking to contrive an ambience so fluid that the most sensitive, withdrawn, imponderable forms could evolve in it without effort. Like an extraordinarily diluted liquid of incredibly refined chromatic luminosity, the medium had the important property of presenting no obstacle to the sympathy between the spectator and the painted forms. Black is almost completely banished from this palette; there is no darkness of shadow; everything in this magical transfiguration is fully apparent, everything is clarity, lightness, and joy. The artist's mastery over his creation had never been so complete; Kandinsky became increasingly the supreme master of the game.

In the last two years of his life, the occasional reappearance of black and dark colors seems, in this context, to have a meaning somewhat similar to the influx of "angels" at the end of Klee's life; it could be a funereal warning. Although the dominant clarity and lightness are still retained, certain paintings of this period, *White Figure* (1943), *Accord* (1943), *Fragments* (1943), *Ribbon with Squares* (1944), surprise the spectator, who can discover an almost tragic atmosphere in them. The forms are generally related to the bright paintings, but they appear to have lost something of their mobility and vitality. The two large figures of *Accord* seem to be phantoms themselves; and the connections established among the objects in *Ribbon with Squares* – the ladder, the flagstones, the circle, the exclamation mark, and the bird's ghost – seem almost hallucinatory.

Although nothing appears to have changed in Kandinsky's style and technique as a whole, the symptoms of a new kind of uneasiness multiply, symbolized in the form of an allegory by the earthquake depicted in *Darkness* (1943). The drama that had been carefully avoided in the paintings where lucid intelligence and balancing of passions exerted strict controls now insinuates itself into compositions which, though not ostensibly tragic, are permeated by the terrible menace that characterizes Klee's "angels." Certain compositions, *Netting* (1942), *The Red Point* (1943), *Light Ascent* (1943), *Thin Threads* (1943), suggest traps in which the body, and especially the soul, risk being caught. Dark backgrounds no longer have the innocent significance that they had in the color drawings of Holland, forty years earlier; now they presage funereal solemnity. Although the picture is small in size, the two great figures of *Accord* take on a hieratic, menacing severity and a monumental, almost gigantic appearance.

CONCLUSION

After examining the development of Kandinsky's art to its final stage of evolution, and observing everything that he created, stated, foretold, and established as a solid and fruitful foundation in which the art of the future could find its sources, inspiration and tutelage, one must conclude that every experiment of contemporary painting was already tried by him. He knew and applied every possible means of liberating the concrete, even attempting so-called formless art, which is perhaps the result of abstraction carried to its final conclusion. The concrete was for him what others call abstract, that is, the absence of forms already existing in nature. The concrete is that which exists before the differentiation of natural phenomena; it is life in its essence, at its source, pure energy not yet limited and contained by form. The concrete to which Kandinsky resorts is primordial reality, that which must be abstracted if it is to be freed from the concealing and oppressive weight of the accidental.

The history of Kandinsky and his painting is the story of his moving search for the essential by way of the emotions and the contemplation of objective forms, until at last he could capture each essence in an image, at the core of which it lives as at the heart of a living being. This story could be told only briefly here, to illustrate some of the principal points through which the course of his life passed and display some of its highlights. "Whosoever buries himself in the depths of his art, in quest of invisible treasures, works to raise a spiritual pyramid that will reach the sky," said Kandinsky. It is for us to follow him in this search for "invisible treasures" and to recognize them in the plastic transformations he created in his quest.

BIOGRAPHICAL NOTES

1866   Kandinsky born in Moscow, December 4.

1886   Studies at University of Moscow.

1889   To Vologda with ethnographic group. First trip to Paris.

1896   Moves to Munich and begins study of painting.

1901   Founds Phalanx group, which holds first exhibition.

1902   Exhibits with Phalanx, Munich and Secession, Berlin.

1903–05 Travels to Venice, Odessa, Moscow, Tunis, Holland, Rapallo.

1905   Exhibits at Salon d'Automne, Paris.

1906   Stays one year at Sèvres, near Paris.

1907–08 Berlin. Various exhibitions.

1909   Munich. *Neue Künstler Vereinigung.*

1910   First abstract watercolor. Writes *On the Spiritual in Art.* Meets Franz Marc.

1911   With Marc, founds Blaue Reiter, which holds exhibition in Munich.

1912   First retrospective exhibition in Munich.

1913   Exhibitions in Berlin and Amsterdam.

1914   Leaves for Russia, where he stays until 1921.

1922   Invited to join the Bauhaus in Weimar.

1926   The Bauhaus leaves Weimar for Dessau and Kandinsky follows.

1932   The Bauhaus suppressed by the government.

1933   Kandinsky moves to Paris, where he remains to the end of his life.

1944   Dies at Neuilly, December 13.

LIST OF ILLUSTRATIONS